I0531250

A Park Stands on All of Our Graves

A Poetry Collection

Khadijah Z. Ali-Coleman

DEDICATION

This poetry collection is dedicated to the people of Palestine, the descendants of Black people enslaved within the American slave trade system, the indigenous people of North America– all of the people who push back against oppression time and time again. May (y)our bodies find rest. May we all be liberated soon.

ABOUT THE AUTHOR

Khadijah Z. Ali-Coleman, Ed.D. is a mother, community organizer and cultural architect with over 20 years of applied experience transforming places into arts and educational spaces. She is award-winning performance artist Khadijah Moon, and a multi-genre writer who is a playwright and filmmaker. She served as the second Poet Laureate of Prince George's County, Maryland from 2023-2025.

Dr. Ali-Coleman is author of the published and forthcoming poetry collections *Halos for Heroes, Friends and a Few People I Don't Like* (2026), *For the Girls Who Do Too Much* (2024), *The Summoning of Black Joy* (2023), the children's book *Mariah's Maracas* (2018) and co-editor of the book *Homeschooling Black Children in the US: Theory, Practice and Popular Culture* (2022).

Dr. Ali-Coleman is founding director of **Black Writers for Peace and Social Justice**, a 501(c)3 nonprofit started in 2024. She founded the multidisciplinary arts group **Liberated Muse** in 2008 and co-founded the national education research group, **Black Family Homeschool Educators and Scholars, LLC (BFHES)**, in 2020, in the midst of the COVID-19 quarantine. BFHES has provided a supportive space for over 3000 families since then, offering annual teach-ins and workshops.

She is an associate professor in the Humanities department at Coppin State University in Baltimore, Maryland.

Praise for *A Park Stands on All of Our Graves*

Khadijah Z. Ali-Coleman's poems explore themes of identity, resistance, social justice, history, culture, and the American machine's cringeworthy hypocrisy. She tenderly examines the political trends/winds with a raw, soulful verse, which begs to be heard. This collection is a unique form of militant jazz. A must read.

-**Synnika A. Lofton,** author of *Monsters in My Head*

Both a meal and a treasure trove of lessons, A Park Stands On All of Our Graves is something to chew on, savor, and swallow...Dr. Ali-Coleman's latest offering, is a dish best served simmering and without an iota of an apology.

~**B. Sharise Moore,** author and poetry editor of FIYAH Magazine of Black Speculative Fiction

A Park Stands on All Our Graves is the rough root medicine we need for what ails us in these menacing times. Searingly honest, two parts witness, two parts critical introspection, and all heart; Ali-Coleman's accessible poems give readers tough questions to ponder like, "How do I resist in the shadow of empire?" and "How am I complicit in its rise? Ali-Coleman's answers may surprise you, invigorate you and indict you, but in the spirit of Ida B. Wells-Barnett, Jayne Cortez and June Jordan, these courageous poems implore you to stop wringing your hands, plant your feet and "jump into a fire/wearing only faith."

-**Derrick Weston Brown,** author of *Wisdom Teeth and On All Fronts; Floodgates Poetry Series Vol.5*

A Park Stands on All of Our Graves

This new poetry collection from Khadijah Ali-Coleman seizes our national crisis and dares to talk back to it. Through evocative haikus and energetic long form poems, she exposes and decries injustice, racism, genocide, and the deliberate erasure of truth. There is passion here and there is also craft.

There is dark wit, as in the rebuke of runaway A.I. in 'Musky Blocks the Sun,' with its intricate rhymes and its mix of standard expression with vernacular. The technical skill and stylistic innovation of Ali-Coleman's poems give depth and authority to her protest. From its haikus to its couplets to its shape verse, this book conveys rage and despair rendered through specific images and precisely controlled language. In this way, she enables art itself to perform the vital task of reclaiming history and identity, of crying 'we are here.'

Khadijah Z. Ali-Coleman is a voice for our time.

-**V. Melissa Holland, Ph.D.**, City of Laurel Arts Council, Prince George's County Arts & Humanities Council

A Park Stands on All of Our Graves is a fierce lament against racism's violence wherever it raises its demon-like head in the world. Replete with compelling form play, it is also a haunting charge to resist the subtle—and often not-so-subtle—ways victims of racism are conditioned to be collaborators in their own coffin measurements. Indeed, in the poem "Because I Do Not Want to Be Complicit," she writes, "Palestine is our mirror, / a forecast of our later, / a dusting of our now, / a barometer of our yesterday." In America, in the early 21st century, it takes courage to make this point—and to do so with unapologetic boldness. Ali-Coleman accomplishes this in her poetry with depth, craft, and emotional authenticity—out loud.

- **Truth Thomas**, Inaugural Poet Laureate of Howard County, Maryland

A Park Stands on All of Our Graves

ACKNOWLEDGMENTS

I would like to acknowledge all of the people who have been unyielding in their forward-facing work in bringing awareness to the conflict in Gaza. I would like to publicly acknowledge the tireless work of activists like Noura Erakat, Saul Williams, Amanda Seales, Qasim Rashid, and Greg J. Stoker and others who continue to use social media in a way to keep people informed, galvanize global support and consistently speak truth to power since before October 7, 2023. I hold high appreciation for media outlets like Democracy Now! that do not bend towards yellow journalism and continue to cover global news honestly and consistently despite the current war on journalists. It has been a saving grace to access these voices during these tumultuous times.

I would like to thank my daughter, Khari and my partner, Ben, for their ever-present support when it has come to my packed schedule which has sometimes impacted our family time. Thank you for your patience and love. Thank you to the establishments that have hosted readings of my work from this collection and to the readers of drafts that have offered their generous support by providing blurbs and feedback. Special thanks to B. Sharise Moore, Derrick Weston Brown, Synnika Lofton, and, V. Melissa Holland.

I would like to thank the following editors and publications for publishing poems within this collection early on, as well as the event curators and venues that featured me, allowing me to work before publishing: Tom Hirons of *Clarion,* Truth Thomas of The *Skinny Journal*, Drew Anderson of Spit Dat open mic at Woolly Mammoth Theater, Furious Flower Poetry Center 2024 Conference, and the Kennedy Center Millennium Stage.

A Park Stands on All of Our Graves

CONTENTS

A Park Stands on All of Our Graves

Park Stands on All of Our Graves

It is poisoned ivy that clings to the mantle,
dances in the parlor,
readies its dress
for the banquet that begins at nine.

In its own honor, it plants trees for dinner
guests,
Europe's finest firs to ravage the land.
The plumes of smoke curl like feathers
tucked in a flapper's headband

As the cries of dead children melt
into the sod flung onto their burlap caskets,
a prayer over wine is the charm of a menace,
wondering where next can one plant a blooming
bush.

Soon comes morning
when no one is left to remember the village's
name.
Soon comes nightfall
When no one shall know this here was a village.

The faces of its people sift with the dirt,
mixing with this new earth that will turn into fall,
becoming the echo whistling through foreign
leaves.

Away from the Fans

It is lonely here most times.
Away from the spectacle,

with a courteous view, I feel
resigned and heavy, brow

twisted within a sculptured
furrow. I am unable to detach

the man from his atomic actions,
believe in idyllic words that don't

match applied politics. A bomb
is a bomb is Obama, is Kamala, is

Condoleeza is a nestled cancer
that explodes fire when you are

already running, already fleeing,
already trying to escape death

when you don't know you are
already dead. What is living anyway

when you are always up against
maniacal terrorists who chewed up

your entire family in each lifetime and
now expect you to wear their chattel brands

with a demented smile? I sometimes think
that I want to inch closer, join the crowd,

don a spectator's glazed eye. But,
my throbbing memory keeps intruding,

silencing the threat, moving my lips
in a chanting, casting protection spells

keeping monsters at bay. It knows.
If I get too close, the leveling of spirit

will carry me to the point of no return
where my own hand will push the button.

Ignite a fleeing. Demolish a people.
How do we reach the end of this lifetime
unscathed?

The Algorithm

Enemies are fans
who do not know they are part
of your audience

Musky Blocks the Sun

We can't see the stars in the sky no more.
Musky got his satellites blocking the sun.
Meddling with the universe, skipping recklessly
above,
taking trips and playing tricks with kisses just for
fun.
Praying at the pulpit of drones and driverless
cars,
we are goading enablers,
guilty scavengers who consume without thought,
at the will of AI laborers

listening to our conversation right now,
trying to steal our soul and our art.

(I mean, AI eavesdroppers memorizing our
conversation right now,
trying to mimic our soul and our art.)
(I mean, AI professionals rewriting our
conversation right now
with their new souls and our stolen art.)
Changing the heading and the commas,
changing the sky to your mama, to my mama—

(My mama ain't in the sky no more—)
Ain't no heaven no more.
Musky got his satellites blocking the sun.
The earth is flat with no end in sight.

Wielding his billions like a gun,
a change agent and viral plight.
Stealing Malcolm's X in revenge,

as we shift on our sunken sofas,

surfing channels as we program binge,
our minds collapsing faster than a fallen nova.
Musky got his satellites blocking the sun.
Organized religion has seemingly changed,
taking trips with kisses just for fun.

We are so willfully engaged
in this everyday circus,
addictive clicks and swipes for laughs,
swapping ill-informed opinions for priceless
researched facts.
Outside they bomb another country,
and keep raising the price on gas.
Over there they designing a new currency,
as we bleed our coffers and sacrifice our
firstborn.
Musky got his satellites blocking the sun,
as the ice keeps melting and the days keep
getting too warm.
The download is inevitable, the rewrite will be
epic.
We will replay this moment, only to rewind and
then forget it.
Musky got his satellites blocking the sun,
meddling with the universe, taking trips with
Bezos for fun.
We copying his game plan, making efforts to try
and win.
Musky and the gang have already won. Yet, here
we go again.
Musky got his satellites blocking the sun,
and it's getting harder to see the moon.

The sky will be invisible sooner than later as we
are stranded earthbound,
craving to become celestial maroons.
Meddling with the universe, skipping recklessly
above,
Musky got his satellites blocking the sun.
Bumping fists with orange knuckles, breathing
vapor of a dying planet.
Into the blackness he has run.
And, yet it's like we still don't understand it.
Musky got his satellites blocking the sun.
I can't see the North Star no more.
I thought I'd ask and take a class to help me
know why.
But, I just learned that just yesterday,
Musky done gone and bought the whole
goddamned sky.
Musky got his satellites blocking the sun,
in the sky that he owns and where he now lives,
leaving the earth to decay and rot and
self-harm,
as the waters rise and the heat singes.
Musky got his satellites blocking the sun,
as his spaceship goes higher and he looks down,
waving goodbye.
What will it be like for you and me when we can
no longer see the sky?
What will it be like for you and me when we can
no longer see the sky?

The Way They (Don't) Speak of Us

It's as if we are imaginary
Wisps of outspoken flares

That signal nothingness
As if our voices were attached

to the aftermath of a demolition site,
Sunken and cratered in barren earth

But, the mother is never absent,
Even if her body is no longer there.

We manifest the seed, the root,
The leaves and the blossom.

The very dirt is of our skin
In the folds of our breath,

The blessing and the curse.
There is no pivot on this wretched rock
Without the cry of the mother.

Whether birthing or burying,

Saving or surrendering,
Watching or weeping,

Our memories are the fabric
of each rotation towards all that is anew.

All that is imaginable.

A Park Stands on All of Our Graves

Although they wish we were imaginary,

From our lungs blare the fury of the muses.
Our pens scribble and our hands clamor

to paint and sculpt what we feel
and know before we forget that We Are Real.
Each revolution is our calling.
In the cycles and the milestones

We have stood alone, and, sometimes
Side by side the very ones who slander our
name,

Who erase us from the canon of truth.
But, we grow everlasting,

Demanding from each day an answer,
an awakening and a reminder

as night promises us gilded legacy
within a galaxy of stars refusing their fall

Delusion

Palestine is free
but colonizers resist
their reality

Blood & Make-Up

Before I was born
there has been
a million women
                    and more
who lived before
and none of them
whispered in my ear
to warn me that
being a woman
would mean bleeding
    all the time

and being in pain
    all the time   because
you are bleeding

No one told me
I would become a
gaping blood faucet
Dripping loudly
my panties a bucket

a sopping mess
one achingly long period
of time
each month
except

when housing a baby, or
when something
                    that shouldn't be
is growing in my uterus
is growing
and they gotta cut it out,

11

a gaping hole, bleeding
            you become

If only
they would have told me

they didn't say
that make-up is
for pretend

the costume you wear
after some man
done hit you
or   before he has
killed you

you pat it on to hide
unsettled tears leaking
from a heart that
rattles in its brokenness
        ignored because
no one
really listens
or cares   about your sorrow

because
either
they are a woman
    who is in pain, too

or a man
who does not
see you as human
in the same way
he sees himself

        This make-up hides well.

If only
one of those
million or so
before me
had prepared me
for this life
of endless waiting
and wanting

of bleeding
and brushing
on a fresh face
to find safety
from this inadequacy
of aloneness,
vulnerable in a world
                    run by men

When She Leads Her People
(Into the Arms of a Monster)

She is smiling
and laughing and looking like us
and sounding like us
and knows our secrets and
where the bodies have been hidden
but she won't share her secrets.
won't tell us how much she traded
to sprinkle bombs, translate the colonizer's
language into a convincing Blaccent,
Cuz "They not like us, They not like us,
They not like us,"
and neither is she,
while swimming in genocide-colored circles,
saluting a foreign flag.
She is dancing

and clutching pearls of the rosary
as she sacrifices us to
a hungry orange monster,
who sweats the red of
a confederate flag
and builds a Dixie prison
near cotton.
She dismisses these monsterly
Things, knowing that Monsters will Monster.
And, she is off-duty,
off-camera, writing
pages for a book she will
sell with our blessings
with our skulls at her feet
and our votes in her pocket

as she murmurs in HBCU and
hallelujah, and #BlackLivesMatter
She is shining

Her pointed star badge
and giggling in war crimes and
military contracts,
grabbing a coffee on the veranda,
watching the smooth dulcet
tones of emptiness as waves
crash into sunset
and rotten ice floats, drowning
immigrant dreams and Gen-Z futures,
as armed militia drape American cities
in the quiet of the night,
guns trained on our backs, filled
with the bullets she has blessed
with her silence

Presidential Candidate Attire

an angry dance of a man,
slick
oily
messiness.
entitled
slick.
mediocrity
drenched
in
slick.
an angry dance of a man.

Death to the Dreamers
(Martin Luther King Blvd, USA)

Poverty looms nakedly
Unashamed by its damage,
its sagging grayness that leeches
into the cracks of walls still standing,

Skipping over stars that have dropped from the
sky,
Laughing, Pointing, Unmerciful
merriment heaves its filthy breath
onto the breaking necks of each passer-by,

Hurling its heavy legs
and stomping on each tendril of a perhaps,
a maybe, a why not?
As aromas of despair circle,
sirens slice the air.

Ringmasters select riders
for this macabre merry-go-round;
sharpening shining badges. The noose
hangs daintily for those fortune has forgotten

While a coffin sits in an unmanned car,
broken parts of a fallen tree crumbling inside
church doors open, emptying the streets,
offering the grieving wails of a mother
as its last communion

Because I Do Not Want to Be Complicit

I write this poem
because my spoken words
will disappear soon,
and this poem will be
my paper trail,

my public dissent,
my scream
and shout
pushing incessantly
through my stapled lips

I write this poem
as I watch the soaking
of my tax dollars
in the blood of
humans fleeing for their lives

because of decade-long lies
of fabricated entitlement and
xenophobic indoctrination
and because my arms
are not long enough,

my voice is not strong enough
to catch a bomb and
toss it back to sender. I cannot
swallow a vulgar sniper's bullet,
nor toss aside a grim reaper wearing
helicopters from strings that hover and drop
death,

I write this poem

wearing skin and muscle,
nerves that sometimes stop working.
Useless tears
that cannot even send water.

I write this poem
with hopelessness that feels stiff
and jagged, a useless shank
that cannot find the artery
that keeps giving life to an uneven deading.

A war with only one side
with weapons. Only one side with honor.
With morals and courage
even when there is no food
nor shelter from a falling sky.

I write this poem
to an immoral war, a treacherous
massacre that is funded by
my helplessness, mocking
my paralyzed intention each day as it slaughters
children without pause.

I write this poem
as it laminates October 7th
as a death date, circles it on its calendar,
chugging its beer, sliding stolen olives
down its gluttonous throat,

designing its future that will stand
on the graves of martyrs, sleeping in
beachfront settlements built on
pristine sands as bodies are swept away
trying to make us forget again where the

demons dwell.

I write this poem
blinded by fury, unable to see
through the smoke. Trying to see
if there is a future
and wonder where in it I will stand.

The world has watched death before,
seen the very end of days
for George, Sonya and Oscar. Heard it come for
Trayvon.
Saw the bombs drop on 6221 Osage Avenue.
And, there were no poems to save them.

No words to drape over the flowing blood
and bodies of murdered children
and youth who did not realize
their morning smile would be their last.
No poems to scream at Black folk

to remind us that Palestine is our mirror,
a forecast of our later,
a dusting of our now,
a barometer of our yesterday.
I write this poem to acknowledge that.

I write this poem
to acknowledge that my solidarity
lies in the trauma and disrupted nervous system
that knows no rest.
Has received no apology.

I write this poem
as another casualty

on the other side of the world
who has not chosen death
but is forced every day to be complicit in its
making.

Healing Word

Patience rarely bleeds.
It is a clotted knowing
that better will come

Travel Advisory

Enter at your own risk.
Hide your valuables.
Tuck your cultural artifacts into that secret
pocket in your checked bag.

Seal the bag up.
Don't you wear grandma's land on your back.
Keep your mother's tongue out your mouth,

You in America now.
Don't you let loose of your father's Gods,
for this country will kill them quick,

will pluck them from their thrones,
and heave them in an apron before they can
Escape

A vat of grease awaits.
Will you have fries with your burger?
The death toll lurks nearby and wonders.

Will it be diabetes?
A school shooting?
Or, a sunny walk in front of an idle driver that will
meet you at the gates?

A stamping of a passport thunders nearby
And she asks,
Do you have anything to declare?

The Eclipse

I wish for a steady heart.
One that does not know fear of empty shelves
nor,
the roaring anger of fist landings.
Pushing the heart to run faster than it is ready.
Both revel in leaving prints that
paint messy on your memory.
Today, I stared into the sun before
the moon hid it from view and I wished
for lightness that can never be darkened,
can never wear heavy again.
And it smiled back and said, "done."

When Zombies Bully

Groupthink leads weak wills
to pounce on the first sign of
life they don't possess

HowQuickly
(a reaction to the reactions of Trump's 2nd
presidential win)

It is now
that we realize
how easily our skin tears,
How uneven our walk leans
when we discard
heavy duplicity
without reciprocity.
Our sin is
a blind eye disregarding
a trampling of Ma'at's Law
a salivating fawning
over the grim robes
of the cheating oligarch.
How quickly the tears
of our absent conscience flow,
mixing with the laughing blood
and jeering echoes
Of the headless Martyrs
who chuckle at our audacity

Ticking Hands

I float. atop this desecrated land, unable to
settle, touch down on earth,
for, there is no solid in the ground. nothing
steady to hold us stable.
no soft landing. We Are.   flimsy pawns on a
thrown chess board,

Falling, Falling.

And, my countrymen, who neither I nor time has
absolved of all the sins,

Failing, Failing.

And, my descendants, the daughters and sons of
stolen men who become the favorite pets of their
mother's rapists,

Flailing, Flailing.

And, my traitorous captors, who place the
highest badge of honor on the chest of those
most capable of the most heinous treachery to
humanity,

Oh, the insanity!

We Sit. on ticking hands that never move.
    time stuck in purgatory. Prisoners.
caught by the parishioners of hate, desperate to
prolong all that snatches mercy from its rest.

When We Speak of Palestine

We are told that we should not.
That we do not know what we are
saying. That we are foreigners and

uneducated on the history of the land,
In the history of a struggle.That we do
not know the full story. But, we who are

descendants of a colonized people, Who
have the faded chattel brands still
engraved in our skin know history. We

know the cryptic silence when our
oppression shall not be named. When
government policy enforces our segregation.

When history books erase the existence
of our towns that were bombed, and
drowned and massacred. Lands only to

be handed to the terrorists who are never
named.
Never called out and reminded daily of the
atrocities they have invoked.

When we speak of Palestine, we speak from
the knowing of the flagging exhaustion of
having
to announce your humanness. Pray for the
safety

to leave your home at night and return alive.

Arm
your children with enough love and
encouragement
to build them up just enough so that they don't
intimidate,

so they don't get too anything that might justify
their murder.
When we speak of Palestine we speak about the
state
sanctioned violence that we know all too well.

We call it out when we cry for
Oscar Grant,
For Tamir Rice,

Mike Brown,
Philando Castille,
Freddie Gray,

and the names that did not make their way to an
activist sign.
When we speak of Palestine, we know
what we are speaking of. Of war funds

materializing before health care and schooling
and
safe neighborhoods. We speak of armed militia
in schools whether we call them security

or the police. We know of what we speak.
We know that when we are told not to speak, not
to name a thing,
that we are being demanded to be complicit in
our oppression.

We know that our silence is the gateway to the
repetition of the violence that all of my ancestors
have seen in their lifetime,
the violence that has disrupted each decade of
my own.

When we speak of Palestine, we are speaking
into power
the want for occupation, colonization, violence
and
destruction to end so that our children will know
peace.

Infinite
A poem for Troy Davis

Bits of information about his life floated like
ripped pieces of gossamer
along the wind tunnel formed between mouths
and fingers on keyboards,
tap, tap, tapping his name out in full standing

Troy Anthony Davis

lived. unevenly in the minds of those outside
composed from a collage of recanted
testimonies, dusty memories and clipped quotes,
he breathed but for a moment on the outside his
prison, slowly pieced together,
glued incohesively together from tears, pleas
and acknowledgements on his behalf.
His name tethered to the emblem of injustice.
Red, white and blue. Stars falling.

31

Midnight Marauders

In the dark, they slay
because they do not have soul
Or respect for night

Something is in the Water

And I name it Death.
Death is always freezing. Always freeing.
The bones of my ancestors' kin lie deep in this
ocean.
particles of the floor's ash, moving sediment
washing the water cold. A grave of memories.
I swim in the Atlantic Ocean on vacation and
shudder often.
The temperature is a searing knuckle of ice, even
in 85 degree weather.

Irony shapes this cracked mirror of crashing
wave,
reflecting my tumultuous pause from unrelenting
labor;
it seems I cannot escape the history of my
imprisonment.
Lying on this water's sandy edge, I nap casually
amidst the
swooping crash of tide; shrill lullabies of jumping
feet still
carrying in the wind. Where is the plank?
Is there an edge to this ship?

A middling passage into a rounding cycle of
repeated histories, I wonder.

how deep could I jump

before attempting to reach air?

Depravity

Now, it is illegal to protest war
A-S and A-Z is interchangeable
We now write in code   only
Sealing truth in its own rustic tomb
If we are to keep our jobs, we lie.
Voting for colonization
        for genocide
        for death
Deaths
Deading a people's history
Killing off a tree of descendants
Only ancestors
Only ancestors being born
Blooming in this pathway of annihilation
Bombing
Booming
A bounty of fresh kills by the hands of
Whitened pathology
Unapologetic depravity that has peeled the skin
Of oppression from its victims back
And, pasted it onto its own to wear as a cape
Twirling and
Contorting a gluttonous girth of sadism into the
shape of
A David fighting a goliath
They, an abusing behemoth
Guzzling unwilling tax dollars to fund this public
lynching
An unmerciful sea of death
An unwavering extinguishing of life
Holding hands with my country, its amorous

accomplice
Wearing its nametag proudly
Erect in defiant audacity
Mockingly with rancid glee.
We scurry. Aimless prisoners of war.

The Manic's Nudge

A sponsored ad convinced me
I would feel better if I stopped snoring.
Pleaded for me to buy a mouth guard
that will push back my tongue.
I bought it because I think it will help me sleep
but it is my mind, not my tongue
that interrupts my sink into slumber.

As the border between sanity
and insanity recedes
disappearing, words endure
the violent rape and mangling by the
poison-tongued
who craft new enunciations
that rationalize genocide
and starvation,
jostling destruction
amidst a circus of celebration.

Music festivals staged
in the center of Armageddon,
a sadist's sonic symphony. We feed
this demon each day. Razors scrapping
our fingers, we wind
through bloodied timelines
of headless children, we extract
ribbons of lilting vowels that
howl and trill, rumination on humanity,
Are we talking about Hamas still?

Snagging our skin

with our Oscar pins,
are we spinning
and twirling while the explosives
are whirring? Lucid and able while our
economy is destabilized as the billionaires
sell their shares, do we deviate
from the stares of the unalived
who decorate the pages of our scroll?

Nudged to the limits
of our imperfect control,
we find our voices, scratchy
and meek, locked within
an election year that already
screams our defeat.

Too many lives to save,
too many ballots to mark,
too many sharks in sharp
suits to harpoon
and overtake, too many grenades
to evade before it is all too late.

Unwrapping my mouth guard,
I pop it in, it moves my tongue,
then releases my jaw so my throat
no longer releases a snore.
But, my mind, oh, my mind is irate
at this vacant remnant
still standing without a door.

There is a kill switch, I think.

Perhaps, I will pull it.

Will it kill everything
or just me, or the people
who keeps running?
Is it faster than a bullet?
Will it deliver food to the starving
or release the candidates who aren't funded?
Will it turn off the faucet that
keeps capitalism breathing?

Will it attach to another part of our soul
and just keep feeding? Does it metamorph
into a CNN pundit? How do I end this?
I keep writing with no solution, no words
that will suffice. Perhaps, I will try to taper
off and disappear in the echo.
Perhaps, this is the price.

What will we become?
What do we know?
How, how, how…
Why, why, why…
Where, where, where do we go?????

I release this poem gently to this air, floating
adrift to the sky, so that it can consider its
choices: to be freely invisible, to be consumed, or
to die.

Violence Anyway

Nonviolence did not save him
Did not wrap him in armor and protect his bones
and blood and soft heart
Did not live him long enough to see his babies
turn into women turning into mothers and
grandmothers
Sons struggling to follow the footsteps he left in
melting snow
Nonviolence did not save him
Did not love him
Did not shield his eyes from the scattered body
parts of little girls in birmingham bombs
Did not fasten his hands tightly around Coretta's
as raging mobs stormed a bridge
Did not make him a bigger person or more
strategic
Did not sing from telephone receivers filled with
CIA bugs
Did not wrap his lifeless body in robes of royalty
making him more deserving of remembrance
Or palatable for tongues that still skulk behind
closed doors to chatter slurs that betray their
liberal smiles
Nonviolence was a background character in a
story of man growing into himself
Learning his mind, broadening his message and
taking off the blinders of middle class mediocrity
He was outcry and warning
Eloquence and fire-starter
A mobilizing switch moving from the pulpit of the
status quo
Steadying his walk among the people

Claiming liberation he saw rising on the horizon
Welcoming him home

Rules of Mediocrity

Lesser men wear hats
to tout the intelligence
they really don't have

We Give the Guns

We give the guns
To rabid sons
Who wear the skins
Of native ones

Who sample grain
And feast on pain
No grace nor mercy
This deadman's game

We give the guns
And bombs in tons
To war machines
And when it's done

We "thoughts and prayers"
We send fake cares
We dodge and dip on
Streaked entrails

Evade world law
In triumphant awe
While holding close the
Monkey's paw

Martyred souls
Strewn about
Headless mourners
Left inside out

A simple feat

A fattened bully
With padded pockets
and victims' clout

We give the guns
To rabid sons
With blighted skin
Who'll bring the end

Who live to die
With resonant cry
"Right to exist,"
the biggest lie

Ceasefire

Sayid's broken parts lay scattered across the
earth
resting in pockets of red dirt,
nestled alongside worms and maggots
frantic at this sudden disruption of their home

They don't know that war is disruption.
is mass murder
is carnage and blood-bath,
but this is not war
because there are no rules

There is no distinction between a woman
and a man, a baby and a soldier, a corpse
and a boy like Sayid playing soccer
before the bomb was dropped

There are no rules, no whistle that blows
and says stop, it is enough, you have killed
everything in sight. The bags are dripping.
Your watching eyes do not plug the holes.

The incessant leaking across the ground
as the world watches, is visual art. A defiling
moment praising your inaction and wondering
who next will push the button to cease fire.

The Rapture
(aka When They Ask Me How I'm Doing 6.23.22)

Emptiness is rapture
Breathless vagueness
A quickening spanning this endless flatness
This dead earth
Blank & futile
Growling in its insistence
It fills me up, climbs atop my head, spreading
Engulfing stillness & weariness. A suffocation.
A willful blanket of echoes,
Mocking in its bleakness.

The Many Ways We Sink

My throat is desert dry
slurping from a porcelain sink.

Alas, I pray and wonder why.
How much farther must we sink?

A living nightmare we have wreaked,
a butcher's blunder, a bloody sink.

My lows have stumbled, my highs have peaked
with clumsy howls that clatter & sink.

Amidst the turmoil, amidst destruction,
this country's compass does morally sink.

Is bearing witness my only function?
I wash my feet in a blameless sink.

A coward's hero with mottled charm.
He stands on land that begins to sink

A sickly win, unbridled harm.
Pushed overboard to drown and sink.

Election day is finally here.
How deep is this wily sink?

There is no joy. There is no cheer.
Into the doldrums I do sink.

A pick of death or currently dying.

A Park Stands on All of Our Graves

Our difference finally suicided to sink.

It's easy to lose without trying.
In pockets deep, their fingers sink.

Hillary's ribbon or Donald's small hands.
A gold mine will become their bloated sink.

A cut of small cloth. A gargle of sand.
Dip your humanity deeply into the sink.

A flag of mercy flying or a trojan horse pushed
in.
You ignore the rising waters as you sink.

Martyrs haunting softly, sighing with chagrin.
Held captive within a devil's boiling sink.

write a poem

write a poem. write a poem about Black
achievement. Black excellence.
But don't mention reprisals. the rage that burns
buildings. knots ropes. grows fruit.
Strange.

write a poem. write a poem about Black
excellence. Black people. that doesn't mention
uneven pavement and concrete ceilings. a poem
empty of kerchiefs and chain clinks.

rows of cotton and water fountains
for only pink lips

write a poem they say. be sure to wear a smile.
peel the pain off the past and
shove it sharply out of sight. cast out the ghosts
that may mumble and call you Negro on the sly.

write a poem. write a poem they say. celebrate
Langston and Zora. but don't remember the
rough parts. the real parts.
the honest parts.

just the jazz parts
without the horns and piano

take out the blues and the drum. wring it out and
leave the bass by the wayside. write a poem
that speaks the language of colorblindness
and knows how to dance and snap its fingers.

write a poem that is jaunty and capable. has a
strong back. one that doesn't yell or cry or
expect reparations. write a poem that sings in
red, white and blue and doesn't celebrate
Kwanzaa.

write a poem that believes Juneteenth is
unnecessary. a poem that doesn't remember,
that doesn't ask questions. write a poem that is
silent and stupid and happy and content. that
believes in white jesus and can quote scripture

write a poem
write a poem
write a poem
write a poem

write a poem that doesn't know why the caged
bird sings or why a raisin is in the sun. a poem
that is empty of everything and all that is. a
poem that is nothing.

write a poem that is nothing.
That is nothing.
write a poem about nothing at all.

Indigenous People's Day
and a Month of Black History

your mother calls you from the kitchen
needing your help to set the table
you can't sit at
needing your help to serve the soup
that you can't eat
for the guests who own the house
your father built

it takes sturdy bones to carry the weight
of days that celebrate your death,
dodging whiskey breath that chases you
'round the world with its confederate flag
wrapped 'round its shoulders,
promising that it will be nice if you
let it destroy your everything
just one more time
just one more time

but it wasn't the last time   when you watched
it
crumple
your name your religion
your language and your very cells and cook it
all in a pot
and serve it back to you as something else

what flavor do we have here now?
a stale token or a martyr crisp?
the bitter root of carnage has emulsified
with evaporated mercy until
winter bears a new holiday

to help you disappear
    just one more time   as it
acknowledges the land it stole from you
hip hip hooraying your assassinated leader
thanking you for your service
while pinning your beads in its hair
drinking your mother's soup

Courage

What is bravery,
but a jump into fire
wearing only faith

Afterword

What do you say about a world where the killing of children becomes normative? For much of my childhood from middle school to college, George Orwell's book, *1984*, was often referenced as a predictive tome that prophesied the rise of a fascist regime where video cameras monitored the everyday actions of citizens and groupthink prevented the messiness of rebellion and true democracy. Never in my wildest imagination as a teen growing up in the 1990's would I have believed that by my middle age the world would embrace the video cameras with craven addiction. How could I foresee our predilection to watch them with unrelenting salivation as aggressive images and sounds become encoded tattoos in our consciousness, emblazoned in our minds even as we slumber?

Droning advertisements, maniacal motivational speakers grifting with faux empathy, dancing politicians and shattered windows as bombs delete women, men and children from existence as everyday fare? How were we to know this is what we would have become? I literally became sick in November of 2023 after a month of Instagram visuals began to flood my timeline, highlighting the horrors inflicted on the people living in Palestine. Recurring COVID-19 infections and labored breathing surfaced where I felt literally smothered each day. Writing about what I was seeing, hearing and feeling was a small respite.

What do you say about a world where the killing of children becomes normative viewing fodder clicked for likes and shares? You say that it is fucked up. You share this condemnation on your social media timelines. You tell anyone who is within inches about what you know. At every moment to present your work, you mention what it is you see and feel. You try to know more so you don't sound ignorant and you don't misrepresent the situation. You may do all of that or none of it. I did most of that and noticed how people sometimes would shrink back away from me when I made mention of genocide or state-sanctioned violence or if I read a poem about how Palestine is the training ground for US police officers to learn tactics they then bring back to America to inflict on Black people. People weren't ready for all of that. My poems about Black resistance, previously annoying to this sect of folks, were now more palatable than anything having to do with Palestine. I was surprised by how my place of work was even more leery of entering this domain of conversation, even as it was touting itself as a space for Black writers, the writers and creatives who were making the most noise and bringing attention to this plight.

During this time, in October of 2023, I was director of a literary organization and knee-deep in producing an awards show that this organization presented annually. I had been at the job by this time for almost two years and wasn't loving it, but aware that I was doing an excellent job in raising money for the organization and elevating its social profile. It was paying the bills, and I had lots of bills. My daughter was in college in San Francisco on full scholarship. But, that scholarship didn't pay for the off-campus apartment she was living in that required at least $1500 a month from me to maintain. This job, which wasn't paying for my health insurance, offered a paltry stipend to use for health needs. That health stipend was added to the pot for my daughter's rent, utilities and groceries. I was miserable daily, showing up to a job I did not like, but I rationalized that this job was helping to fill a gap as I was responsible for two households as my daughter, an excellent scholar and creative writer, was finishing her third and final year of university.

I was really good in the role I had at this job. I had been an administrator in various spaces by this point for over two decades. In less than two years, I had raised almost half a million dollars for this nonprofit in grants and corporate sponsorships and had designed year-round virtual and in-person programming that had never been offered before. The organization was typical of many Black founded nonprofits where their existence had been reliant on the free labor of dedicated volunteers and low-paid staff for the majority of their existence. This often happens because of the racialized realities of nonprofit funding and the tendency for the beneficiaries of Black organizations to not give back financially as readily as they receive the services and support. This is the plight of historically Black colleges and universities as well, not just nonprofits. This is typically due to the reality of the majority of Black people just trying to survive day to day, living paycheck to paycheck to pay for the expenses that always add up. Coupled with systemic racism impacting job insecurity and toxic work environments, many Black people lack the financial safety net that includes disposable income to give to charity organizations and Black-serving institutions.

But, this lack of financial support leaves our institutions vulnerable. This lack of funding often leads to high turnover and the loss of knowledge leaders who contribute to the continuity of programming and stakeholder relationships. This pattern also keeps the organization mired in a start-up-like capacity instead of having the foundational girth to grow and expand. When I was hired by this organization, the hiring committee did not disclose how much was to be done. There was no payroll system, there were no operational standards, and no functioning committee that managed the fundraising and fiduciary health of the organization. I had been told during the interview that my primary responsibility would be programming. I began my job having to build infrastructure.

In less than three months, I had put together a team that was charged with helping build the foundation necessary for programming to happen. However, numerous negative experiences led me to making my mind up that it would only be a matter of time before I would be looking for a new place of employment once my daughter graduated. I also was feeling conflicted, as an artist and an administrator. My art is reliant on me speaking truth to power. Being in a position of responsibility at this particular organization required an allegiance to building relationships that weren't necessarily aligned with my moral compass. I didn't realize I would be shifting so fully into my necessary walk so soon.

So, shortly after the awards show in October, where an awards presenter acknowledged Palestine and many in the audience stood in applause, I was reminded that where I worked, no one had anything to say regarding Palestine. In fact, several of the board members were leaving or not showing up for board meetings and I was being blocked by the active members from recruiting new board members. At the start of 2024, exhausted, I had articulated that I could not go into 2025 with the same board that did not assist with fundraising (there was no fundraising committee), or did not articulate a statement about where they stood on Palestine. Social media was blasting and condemning other mainstream literary organizations for their leadership erring in their support of a country committing genocide.

A break in this wave of fatigue for me was being accepted as a Watering Hole Poetry fellow in 2023 and attending their winter retreat in South Carolina's Santee State Park where I wrote a few of the poems in this collection. A balm to my soul was being able to study under Quraysh Ali Lansana who was mentored by the great Gwendolyn Brooks. He imparted so much wisdom that I felt was being passed down from Ms. Brooks and affirming my work on this manuscript.

The next month, at the start of 2024, I had the opportunity to travel to Cuba for the first time through a group trip coordinated by Andy Shallal, owner of the renowned restaurant chain, Busboys and Poets, popular in Maryland, Washington D.C. and Virginia. Shallal had sponsored the creation of a sculpture made in Cuba to honor Langston Hughes on his 132nd birthday. The trip was organized to bring a delegation of Americans to Cuba to honor Hughes with the iconic author Alice Walker slated to lead the unveiling of the sculpture.

Being in Cuba and seeing the direct impact of global sanctions on their economy was sobering. The diabolical embargo has crushed their economy in a palpable way. But, like the Palestinian people, the Cuban people's strength is steely and indomitable. Their innovation and creativity can not be outdone. I was heavily encouraged to write while on this trip, writing the poem, "Black Is," while in Cuba on my second day and later sharing it publicly during the sculpture unveiling ceremony. That poem and a few other poems written during this time will be featured in my forthcoming collection, *Halos for Heroes, Friends & A Few People I Don't Like.*

Award recipients from the organization I worked were speaking out in solidarity with Palestine and speaking out against the money from American taxpayers being used to fund bombs destroying Gaza and its people. The board at my place of employment remained silent. I know it was largely due to fear of alienating donors who would have looked at any form of solidarity with Gaza as being offensive. On the Cuba trip, I listened to Alice Walker tell us how important it is for us to cultivate our humanity. I learned, while on that trip, the extent of her activism. I had no idea that she had traveled on flotillas for peace in Palestine and the range of her international work. Her presence was an inspirational blessing while in Cuba.

I wrote approximately 20 poems in one week about all of the things I was witnessing, experiencing and synthesizing. I was realizing how much I didn't know I didn't know. I also realized how propaganda had impacted me in ways that I didn't realize. All of these epiphanies came at unexpected moments. They had to come out in some way.

I shared poems on social media, in conversation, at open mics, at readings I had been invited to read at, during podcast interviews and privately at home with my partner and daughter. The helplessness I felt watching all of this unfold and being entrapped in a job situation where I did not feel I was contributing to the world, but instead felt that I was promoting a neoliberalism agenda with the organization's silence, was overwhelming. I left the organization in April 2024 and started the nonprofit Black Writers for Peace and Social Justice a month later.

Without a clear business plan, I decided to use intuition to guide what direction I would go in with nonprofit. I knew I wanted to support writers speaking truth to power. More importantly, I wanted to publicly represent a space where truth was centered and operations weren't reliant on possibly alienating a donor who favored Gaza's oppressors. But, after a week, a business plan was necessary and discipline was necessary to be as dedicated to building this new organization as I had been with the previous job where it was not in sync with my values or life mission.

Through this new nonprofit, immediately I began to present workshops titled, "Writing for Liberation," and developing a pedagogy around writing truth to power. Within the first six months, I had also developed a youth development summer program for high school students and implemented a mountain retreat for Black women writers over 40. I needed to find spaces to attend to finishing this manuscript and realized I needed to create and cultivate these spaces.

Since starting to write the collection, several prominent Black writers began to pass away as well, leaving huge voids in their absence. Some of those writers include activist Assata Shakur, iconic poet Nikki Giovanni, multidisciplinary artist Malcolm Jamal-Warner, and community-based poet Reuben Jackson. I was still reeling from the 2023 death of one my favorite writers and thinkers, Randall Robinson, who died in March of that year. The poems in this book have been written as a form of witness over the course of that year and later, although the world's attention seemed to be triggered with the conflict that exploded on October 7, 2023. Those of us who know history know that the persecution of the people of Gaza did not start on this date. But, this date unlocked something in the consciousness of America that had been generally silent and unaware of the atrocities hurled at the people of Palestine since the 1940's when their land was first seized and the effort to push them out of their land began.

The parallels to the experience of the indigenous people of the United States and the people of African descent throughout the diaspora were uncomfortably triggering. The poems that fell out of me for the next two years after 2023 were angry and direct. Many were soft and wet from my tears as I wrote them.

How could I not think of the Black people of Seneca Village in 1800's New York who were displaced by what is now Central Park in New York City? How could I not think of the multi-cultural community destroyed during the MOVE bombing in Philadelphia on Osage Avenue in 1985? My own family history roared in the background, laced with memories of my mother's birth mother's rape by a white man while institutionalized, leading to the birth of my mother. It is not surprising that I realized that I had been writing about some of these very things for a while in bits and pieces. A couple of poems written a decade before were placed in this collection as their relevance was remembered, including the poem for Troy Davis.

When connecting with history in the way I did to produce this book, fighting the trauma was an ongoing activity. I was reminded every day of the violence enacted towards the indigenous people who lived on the lands where my neighborhood stands when I drive down streets named "Indian Head," "Piscataway," and "Accokeek." This book of poems bears witness to the sense of helplessness that leaves me ashamed each day that I can't do much more than watch from afar as a people, their land, and their cultural artifacts are obliterated. But, by writing through this, I am understanding that I/we continue to live in a state of terror and tension that has been normalized to the point that we are unaware that our plights are intertwined.

Khadijah Z. Ali-Coleman
November 1, 2025

In the presence of the great Alice Walker while on the Cuba trip

My fantastic companions on the Busboys & Poets
trip to Cuba (2024)

Andy Shallal with Langston
Hughes sculpture in Cuba

Alice Walker with the
Langston Hughes sculpture

With the sculptor of the
Langston Hughes sculpture

Performing my poem
"Black Is" at the sculpture
unveiling

www.ingramcontent.com/pod-product-compliance
Lightning Source LLC
Chambersburg PA
CBHW071201130626
46555CB00004B/1545

*9 7 9 8 9 9 9 0 9 7 1 0 1 *